101 HILARIOUS CHICKEN JOKES & RIDDLES FOR KIDS

Laugh Out Loud With These Funny Jokes About Chickens (WITH 35+ PICTURES)!

Medical Disclaimer: The jokes contained in this book are not intended as a substitute for consulting with your (veterinary) physician. All matters regarding your health, as well as that of your chickens, require medical supervision.

Legal Disclaimer: all images used in this book are designed by Freepik.

Table of Contents

INTRODUCTION

What do you get when you cross a chicken with a Martian?

Answer: *An eggs-traterrestrial!*

Thank you for picking up a copy of '*101 Hilarious Chicken Jokes For Kids*'.

Chickens are some of the **funniest creatures** that walk this **earth**, wouldn't you agree?

I mean, the only other animal that has an *even* funnier walk must be the **penguin!**

It's easy to **laugh out loud** at chickens simply by looking at them, going about their business!

But what to do in those unfortunate hours that are *not* spent in the presence of these **funny, friendly birds**?

Don't worry, I've got you covered!

This book is <u>jam-packed</u> with:

- **100+ hilarious chicken jokes, and**
- **35+ funny illustrations**

Get ready for some serious LOLs!

I grew up on a farm, surrounded by cows, goats, and...chickens! So, I know first-hand how they can bring a smile to your face.

Yet, what I also want you to take away from this book is that **chickens are so much more than comedians**. If you have a couple of your own in your backyard, you know what I mean.

As I explain in my other book, *'Backyard Chickens: Join the Fun of Raising Chickens, Coop Building and Eating Fresh Eggs (Hint: Keep Your Girls Happy!)',* having a few chickens of your own means of course a daily **fresh supply of eggs**. Win!

But chickens are also famous for getting rid of all kinds of bugs and pests. They are very helpful like that.

And one other thing that few ever think of is sitting in your backyard and hearing the chickens just talk to each other: it is **so relaxing** after a day at work!

They have a soft **clucking sound** as they go about their business. It is quite **soothing to the soul**, and if you don't watch out, it can put you right to sleep in that garden swing...

So, with that in mind I hope you will be able to appreciate these wonderful birds even more when you *crack up* (**pun intended!**) about the chicken jokes that are up next.

The jokes in this book will:

- warm your heart
- make you smile, and even
- roar with laughter!

I hope you are ready: **let's have a laugh about chickens!**

101 HILARIOUS CHICKEN JOKES

1.

While mending fences out on the range, a very religious cowboy lost his favorite Bible. He was devastated!

Three weeks later, however, a brown chicken walked up to him, carrying that same Bible in its mouth.

The cowboy was astonished, he couldn't believe it! He took the precious book out of the chicken's mouth, thanked him, went on his knees and exclaimed: "*It's a miracle!*".

To which the chicken replied: *"Not really. Your name is written inside the cover."*

2.

Q: How do baby chickens dance?

A: Chick-to-chick!

3.

A chicken sits in a bar, sipping a whiskey.

A customer walks up to him and says, *"Wow, it's not often that I see a chicken drinking bourbon here!"*

To which the chicken replies: *"Yeah, but that's hardly a surprise at these prices."*

4.

Q: How did the eggs leave the highway?

A: They went through the eggs-it.

5.

One day, a man was driving on a country road when he looked out of the window and noticed a chicken running alongside his car. He was amazed to see the chicken keeping up with him: he was driving 40 mph! So, he accelerated to 50. But the chicken stayed right next to him. Even more astonished, he now sped up to 60 mph, but the chicken not only kept up with, it even passed him!

Then the man noticed something peculiar: the chicken had 3 legs. He decided to follow the chicken and finally ended up at a farm. When he got out of his car and looked around, he was even more shocked: all the chickens on this farm had three legs!

He approached the farmer and asked: "*Why do all these chickens have 3 legs?*"

The farmer replied: "*Well, I figured: everybody likes chicken legs, right? So, I decided to breed a three-legged bird. I'm going to be a rich!*"

Then the man asked him how the chicken legs tasted. Then farmer said, with a sad expression on his face: "*I don't know, I haven't caught one yet...*"

6.

Q: How do monsters like their eggs?

A: Terri-fried!

7.

Psychiatrist: What seems to be the problem?

Patient: I think I'm a chicken.

Psychiatrist: How long has this been going on?

Patient: Ever since I came out of my shell.

8.

Q: What does a chicken have in common with a band?

A. Drumsticks.

9.

Returning from the market, the farmer's son was dropped the crate of chickens his father had entrusted to him. The box broke open, and the chickens scurried off in different directions.

The boy panicked for a few seconds, but then quickly got back to his senses. Determined not to disappoint his father, he walked all over the neighborhood scooping up the wayward birds and returning them to the repaired crate.

Finally, the boy – reluctantly – returned home. He hoped he had found them all, but expected the worst.

He felt it was best to just speak up: "*Pa, the chickens got loose,*" the boy confessed sadly, "*but I managed to find all twelve of them.*"

"*Well, you did really well son,*" the farmer replied. "*You left with only seven this morning!*"

10.

Q: Which side of a chicken has more feathers?

A. The outside.

11.

Q: Why shouldn't you tell an egg a joke?

A: Because it might crack up!

12.

Q: How does a chicken tell time?

A: One o'cluck, two o'cluck, three o'cluck...

13.

The chicken farmer died under mysterious circumstances.

The police suspect fowl play.

14.

Q: What does a mixed-up hen lay?

A: Scrambled eggs!

15.

Q: What do you get if you cross a cocker spaniel, a poodle and a rooster?

A: Cockerpoodledoo!

16.

Q: Why does the chicken bring toilet paper to the party?

A: Because he is a party pooper.

17.

Q: Why did the chicken cross the ocean?

A: To get to the other tide.

18.

A first-grade teacher was telling her students the story of the 2005 animated movie 'Chicken Little.' She got to the part when Chicken Little ran up to the farmer, saying: "*The sky is falling. The sky is falling.*"

Then the teacher paused, looked around the class, and asked the kids what they thought the farmer said in reply.

One little boy raised his hand and said: "*I think the farmer said: Holy cow, a talking chicken!*"

19.

Q: What do you call a scary chicken?

A: A poultrygeist.

20.

Q: Where are chicks born?

A: In Chick-cago.

21.

Q: Where do tough chickens come from?

A: Hard-boiled eggs!

22.

Q: What chicken can jump higher than a tree?

A: Any chicken can jump higher than a tree, trees can't jump.

23.

Q: Why did the chewing gum cross the road?

A: It was stuck to the chicken's foot!

24.

Q: Why did the turkey cross the road twice?

A: To prove he wasn't chicken!

25.

A man runs into the office of a psychiatrist and says: *"Doctor, you have to help me: My wife thinks she's a chicken and I don't know what to do!"*

The psychiatrist, still somewhat shocked from the man bursting into his room: *"Ehm, I see. How long has she had this condition?"*

"Two years," says the man.

"Two years, you say?! Then why did it take you so long to come and see me?" asked the psychiatrist.

The man shrugs his shoulders and replies: *"We needed the eggs."*

26.

Q: Why did the chicken cross the playground?

A: To get to the other slide.

27.

I hate winter.

I always feel so cooped up.

28.

Q: What do you get when a pig and a chicken bump into each other?

A: Ham and eggs!

29.

I ate an omelet for breakfast but I'm still feeling peckish.

30.

Q: Why did the chicken go up the stairs?

A: She was already across the street.

31.

One day, a chicken walks into a library. He goes up to the librarian and says "*book book.*" The librarian gives him two books and he walks away.

The next day, the chicken walks up to the librarian again and says "*book book.*"

The librarian wonders what the chicken is doing with the books, so she follows him out the door and to a pond.

The chicken held up the books to a frog and the frog said, "*Red it, red it...*"

32.

Q: What do you get when a chicken lays an egg on top of a barn?

A: An egg roll!

33.

Q: A rooster laid an egg on a barn roof. Which way would it roll?

A: Roosters don't lay eggs, hens do!

34.

Mum: *"Eat your roast chicken, it's got iron it!"*

Son: *"No wonder it is tough!"*

35.

Q: Why didn't the chicken cross the road?

A: The butcher was on the other side.

36.

Shush! I'm hatching a plan. Says the pet chicken heading home to roost.

37.

Q: What did the cat say to the chicken?

A: Check meow-t!

38.

Q: Why did the rooster cross the road?

A: He wanted to impress the chicks!

39.

Q: What do you call a dirty chicken that crosses the road and crosses back again?

A: A dirty double crosser.

40.

Martin Luther Chicken Jr. said: "*I dream of a world where chickens can cross roads and not be questioned of their reason!*"

41.

A chicken went to the post office to send a telegram. He took out a blank form and wrote: "*Cluck. Cluck. Cluck. Cluck. Cluck. Cluck. Cluck. Cluck. Cluck.*"

When he was done, he gave it to the clerk. The clerk looked at the paper and said to the chicken: "*There are only 9 words here. We have a special offer: You could send another 'Cluck' for the same price.*"

To which the chicken replied: "*Sorry, but that wouldn't make any sense at all!*"

42.

Knock, knock!
Who's there?
Doughnut.
Doughnut who?
Doughnut take my eggs, or I'll peck you!

43.

Knock, knock!
Who's there?
Chicken.
Chicken who?
Chicken your pockets, maybe your keys are
there!

44.

Knock, knock!
Who's there?
Omelet.
Omelet who?
Omelet smarter than I look!

45.

Q: Did you hear about the chicken who invented the knock knock joke?

A: She won the no-bell prize!

46.

Two chickens are sitting on opposite sides of a river. One chicken yells to the other: *"How do I get to the other side of the river?"* The other chicken replies: *"You ARE on the other side!"*

47.

Q: What do you do if a chicken pecks at your dictionary and chews the pages?

A: Take the words right out of his mouth!

48.

Q: What happened to the chicken that swallowed a firefly?

A: It barked with de-light!

49.

Q: What does the chicken say to get across a busy street?

A: Eggs-cuse me please!

50.

A policeman in Los Angeles stops a man in a Mustang with a chicken in the front seat.

"What are you doing with that chicken?" he asked, *"You should take it to the farm."*

The following week, the same policeman sees the same man with the chicken again in the front seat. This time, both of them are wearing sunglasses.

The policeman pulls him over again, upset: *"I thought you were going to take that chicken to the farm!"* The man replied: *"I did. We had such a good time we are going to the beach this weekend!"*

51.

Q: Why do Chicken Vampires believe everything you tell them?

A: Because they're suckers!

52.

Q: Why can't a rooster ever get rich?

A: Because he works for chicken feed!

53.

Q: What do you get if you cross a chicken with a cow?

A: Roost beef!

54.

Q: If fruit comes from a fruit tree, where does chicken come from?

A: A poul-tree!

55.

A chicken walks into a job center. "*Wow, a talking chicken*," says the clerk. "*With your talent, I'm sure we can find you a gig in the circus.*"

"*The circus?*" says the chicken, disappointed: "*What does a circus want with a carpenter?*"

56.

Q: Why did the chicken end up in the soup?

A: Because it ran out of cluck!

57.

Q: What do you call a crazy chicken?
A: A cuckoo cluck!

58.

Q: Why did the chicken cross the basketball court?

A: He heard the referee calling fowls.

59.

Q: Why is it easy for chicks to talk?

A: Because talk is cheep!

60.

Q: Why did the chicken cross the road half way?

A: He wanted to lay it on the line!

61.

Q: What do chicken families do on Saturday afternoon?

A: They go on peck-nics!

62.

Q: Why didn't the chicken skeleton cross the road?

A: Because he didn't have enough guts!

63.

On a dark night, a burglar breaks into a house.

As he reaches to steal some valuables, he hears a voice say: *"Jesus is watching you."*

Alarmed by the voice, the burglar jumps up and hides behind the curtain. He peaks around the corner but doesn't see anybody.

So, he goes back to the valuables and continues putting them in his bag.

"Jesus is watching you," the voice says once more.

This time, the burglar looks harder and he sees a chicken.

"Who are you?" he asks.

The chicken replies, "*Elijah.*"

"*Wait, what? Who on earth would call a chicken Elijah?*", surprised that the chicken could talk, yet simultaneously relieved he only got busted by a chicken.

"*I don't know,*" says Elijah, "*I guess the same kind of people that would call a Rottweiler Jesus.*"

64.

Q: What happened to the chicken whose feathers were all pointing the wrong way?

A: She was tickled to death!

65.

Q: Why did the chicken go to KFC?

A: He wanted to see a chicken strip.

66.

Q: What do chickens study in school?

A: Eggonomics.

67.

Q: What do chickens grow on?

A: Eggplants!

68.

Q: Why did the chick disappoint his mother?

A: He wasn't what he was cracked up to be!

69.

Q: What does a chicken need to lay an egg every day?

A: Hendurance.

70.

Q: What do you get if you cross a chicken with a cement mixer?

A: A brick layer!

71.

Q: Why does a chicken coop have two doors?

A: Because if had four doors it would be a chicken sedan!

72.

Q: Which day of the week do chickens hate most?

A: Fry-day!

73.

Q: What do chickens serve at birthday parties?

A: Coop-cakes!

74.

Q: How long do chickens work?

A: Around the cluck!

75.

Q: How can you drop an egg six feet without breaking it?

A: By dropping it 7 feet – it won't break for the first six!

76.

Q: How do comedians like their eggs?

A: Funny side up!

77.

Q: What do you call a group of chickens clucking in unison?

A: A Hensemble.

78.

Q: What do you call a bird that's afraid to fly?

A: Chicken.

79.

A chicken was going to America. After he left, her best friend was asked where she was going.

He said "*I don't know, but definitely not to Kentucky!*"

80.

On a Saturday night, a man and his pet chicken were drinking shots a bar. They had started off slowly, watching TV, drinking beers. But as the night progressed, they had moved on to drinking all kinds of shots. Finally, the bartender says: "*Last call!*"

The man says: "*One more for me... and one more for my chicken.*"

The bartender pours the both them their last shot of the night. Suddenly, the chicken falls over dead…

The man throws some money on the bar, puts on his coat and starts to leave. The bartender yells: "*Hey fella, you can't just leave that lyin' there!*"

To which the man replies: "*That's not a lion, that's a chicken.*"

81.

Q: How many eggs can you eat on an empty stomach?

A: Just one, because then your stomach won't be empty.

82.

Why did the chicken cross the road? It's actually a tragic story.

Many years ago, a chicken named Wilma overheard the farmer say: "*If this chicken does not lay eggs we will have to kill her.*"

Petrified, Wilma crossed the road and went to the farmers market. She bought a carton of eggs and raced across the road back to the farm. Since that day, she did this every day, for the rest of her (long) life.

That is why the chicken crossed the road...

83.

Q: What kind of chicken eats with their ears?

A: They all do! Who removes their ears before dinner?

84.

Q: How does a chicken mail a letter to her friend?

A: In a HEN-velope!

85.

Q: Is chicken soup good for your health?

A: Not if you're the chicken!

86.

Q: What happens when you name a chicken after Kim Kardashian?

A: You give a chicken a bad name.

87.

A man sits down in a movie theater and notices what looks like a chicken sitting next to him.

"*Are you a chicken?*", the man asks, surprised. "*Yes,*" the chicken replies.

"*What are you doing here, watching a movie?*", the man asked.

To which the chicken replied: "*Well, I liked the book.*"

88.

Q: What did Snow White call her chicken?

A: Egg white.

89.

Q: What did the eggs do when the light turned green?

A: They egg-celerated!

90.

Q: What do you call a city of 20 million eggs?

A: New Yolk City!

91.

Q: What do you call an egg that goes on safari?

A: An eggs-plorer!

92.

Q: What do you call an excited chicken?

A: Hen-thusiastic.

93.

Q: What did the Spanish egg farmer say to his hens?

A: Oh lay!

94.

Q: What do you call a mechanic who lives on a farm?

A: An egg-chanic.

95.

Q: What do you get when you cross a chicken with a Martian?

A: An eggs-traterrestrial!

96.

Q: What did the chicken say to the flea?

A: Stop bugging me!

97.

Q: What do you call a rooster who wakes you up at the same time every morning?

A: An alarm cluck!

98.

Q: What happens when a hen eats gunpowder?

A: She lays hand gren-eggs!

99.

Q: What happens when you drop a hand gren-egg?

A: It eggs-plodes!

100.

Q: What's more amazing than a talking chicken?

A: A spelling bee.

101.

One day, a man visited his friend. When he walked into the living room, he found his friend playing chess with a chicken.

Astonished, he watched the game for a couple of minutes. "*I can't believe my eyes*!" he exclaimed. "*That is the smartest chicken I have ever seen.*"

To which his friend replied: "*Mwoah, he's not that smart. I've beaten him three games out of five.*"

OTHER BOOKS BY THE AUTHOR

BONUS CHAPTER: WHY KEEP CHICKENS IN YOUR BACKYARD?

This is a bonus chapter from my book **'Backyard Chickens: Join the Fun of Raising Chickens, Coop Building and Eating Fresh Eggs (Hint: Keep Your Girls Happy!)'** *Enjoy!*

***

Backyard chickens are chickens that are kept in an urban setting, usually in one's backyard.

There are many out there that think that if you get chickens that is one more thing to be taking care of at home. But, not so if you manage and set things up the right way.

Raising chickens is very rewarding and a wonderful way to introduce your children to some early farm chores. As a child of about ten, my grandfather purchased twelve chickens for me so that they could lay eggs and I could sell them as a way for me to make money to put back for college. He was teaching me early on how to be frugal.

Chickens make wonderful pets. They are extremely social and very nosey as to what you are doing in your backyard all the time. Chickens have become so popular in Hollywood that a lot of the stars have them for pets in their homes and have designer clothes made for them. With little chicken diapers made to match!

One of the first questions many people ask when it comes to raise chickens is if it is hard and expensive. Worry not: raising a chicken is a breeze. The initial start-up costs some money, but the upkeep afterward is fairly inexpensive.

Let's start with some basics and go from there so you can figure out what will work for you.

***

Raising Chickens Is Cheaper Than You May Think

I feel like having chickens are cheaper than having a dog. And, I have had many dogs, and about every farm animal, you can name growing up on the farm. Their food is cheap, there are all kinds of chicken housing options, ways to water, chicken swings and so forth that can all be made by things you may already have around your house.

I can't think of anything better than going out to the chicken house and gathering eggs, putting them in the basket, coming back in and cooking them for breakfast. The eggs you buy in the store pale in comparison. These come from chickens that have all been housed in a huge long chicken house, with no place to move except their 16 x 16 inch square of mesh and eating, waiting for the time that egg is to pop up and roll down the shaft to be picked up and hauled away to market.

Having chickens in your backyard, and especially if you raise your chicks in the spring, gives you many options. You could either:

- sell the baby chicks
- sell the chickens as they grow
- sell the eggs, or
- process the chicken for the meat to eat yourself

I must confess that last part was a little difficult for me to write as I always wind up making big pets out of the chickens and they wind up living in a chicken nursing home until their time comes to go to that big nest in the sky.

I promise you though, as a child, I helped with many, many chickens as we harvested them for the freezer when they reached the right age.

***

Fresh Eggs. Every Day!

A good chicken will produce eggs for you for about two years and sometimes a little longer. You can tell when she starts to slow down. Her eggs will start to get smaller, and we call that her "henopause" years. She will not lay an egg every day, but every now and then she will lay an egg about half the size of what she used to lay as a young hen.

By raising your chickens, you know what is going into them and what is around them. You will know that they are not being subjected to chemicals, pesticides, growth hormones or antibiotics to keep their food fresh longer. You will know the quality of your eggs, a comfortable feeling to have whether you are eating the eggs yourself or are selling them to your neighbors.

These fresh eggs are also better for your health. You will find more than seven times of Vitamin A and Beta Carotene as well as Vitamin E in your eggs over the grocery store eggs. Your chickens will supply you with 292 mg of Omega 3 while those from the store will give you 0.33 mg. Home grown eggs are lower in saturated fat as well.

***

Chickens are Intelligent and Caring

Chickens are very smart. They also have a great memory and know the difference of over 100, yes, I said 100, human and animal faces. They have feelings too. They dream (don't know how the scientists have proved this, but whatever they say), they mourn for each other, they like to play, and they can feel distress and pain.

They are wonderful mommas. While they are sitting on their eggs waiting for them to hatch, they talk to their babies inside the eggs, and as a worrisome chicken mother will do, the hen will turn her eggs about 50 times a day.

***

Hanging Out With Your Chickens Helps Reduce Stress

There have been studies on the stress reducing effect of kittens and dogs. Just recently, I read about a study showing that cortisol levels dropped appreciably in children who were accompanied by their pet dog when giving a presentation in class.

I am not aware of a similar study on the stress reducing effect of chickens, but let me tell you from personal experience: there is nothing like kicking back at the end of a busy day, with a glass of red Bordeaux wine, and hanging out with the chickens. It is deeply relaxing to tune in to their soft clucking sound as they do their thing.

And they can keep a secret! Seriously, I have shared my deepest feelings and most embarrassing moments with them, and it never came back and bit me in the tail. Although I am pretty sure they gossip about me when I'm not around...

***

Free Manure

A lot of people do not get excited about chicken manure, but our family does. It makes great fertilizer for your flowers and vegetable garden. Put it in the ground below the roots, and you will have some amazing plants that your neighbors will be wondering how you raised such large plants. You can also use your eggshells, but those are also good to give back to your chickens for the calcium which we will talk about later.

The manure great to spread on your lawn, and if you have between five and ten chickens, they should give you about enough fertilizer for your whole yard in a year's time.

***

Chickens are a Great Pest Deterrent

With chickens around, you will not have to buy pesticides if you allow them to free range a little every day. They will eat about any grasshopper, cricket, tick, slug, beetle, tomato worm, flies if they can catch them, and I have even seen them try to peck around on a snake!

They make great gardeners too. You just need to watch out for your ripe tomatoes. They like ripe tomatoes; they like to peck a hole in them, eat a little and go on to another. But they will scratch around and eat the weed seeds that have fallen, helping you with advance weed problems.

***

Chickens Help You Dispose of Your Leftovers

Chickens are great little garbage disposals. They love anything you have left over after a meal. In the winter, when the temperature gets down to freezing, my mother makes sure she cooks them warm food to keep them happy. It seems to work as their production does not slack if she cooks for them. This is a time-honored tradition passed down through the generations to keep your chickens laying well in the winter. They love warm cooked beans or peas.

***

If you must be away for a day or two, I can promise you it is never hard to get a neighbor to watch them, if you promise to let them keep the eggs they gather while you are away.

Don't get me wrong; there will be some initial start-up costs, but all in all, keeping chickens in your backyard is well worth it.

It becomes a great hobby for you and the kids. There are so many kinds of chickens out there to choose from that you just would not believe. And, there are chicken shows, just like dog shows, where you can enter your chickens or your rooster for a prize.

Now, before we move on to chicken coops, let's first take a closer look at the different chicken breeds that you can choose from. Which breed works best for you depends on what you value most. Do you want to keep chickens for show, meat or just their eggs? How you answer that question determines what kind of chickens will enter your coop.

***

This is the end of this bonus chapter.

Want to continue reading?

Then go to the Amazon website and search for "Backyard Chickens"

Hope to see you there!

45185605R00074

Made in the USA
Columbia, SC
20 December 2018